T0193269

WestBow Press books may be ordered through booksellers or by contacting:

WestBow Press
A Division of Thomas Nelson & Zondervan
1663 Liberty Drive
Bloomington, IN 47403
www.westbowpress.com
844-714-3454

Because of the dynamic nature of the Internet, any web addresses or links contained in this book may have changed since publication and may no longer be valid. The views expressed in this work are solely those of the author and do not necessarily reflect the views of the publisher, and the publisher hereby disclaims any responsibility for them.

Any people depicted in stock imagery provided by Getty Images are models, and such images are being used for illustrative purposes only. Certain stock imagery © Getty Images.

ISBN: 979-8-3850-1505-4 (sc)
ISBN: 979-8-3850-1507-8 (hc)

Library of Congress Control Number: 2023923954

Print information available on the last page.

WestBow Press rev. date: 01/17/2024

REFLECTIONS
AND
TREASURED
WONDERS

Written and illustrated by

MARGARET KOHEL EVANS

This book is dedicated to my father,
Benedict Kohel.

Dancing
the joy of
life sets my
soul on fire.

Beach Run at Sunset
Watercolor 2023
Wild horses are unique on Assateague Island which is split between Maryland and Virginia. There is one herd on each side, and they frequently run the beach. A delight to see!

Listening
is spiritual
attentiveness.

Meadowlark
Watercolor 2021
The Western Meadowlark's unique pure gurgles and tones are easily remembered from early childhood. They sing various songs: all beautiful to the ears.

2

Rejoicing in the gift of life is a daily tribute.

Barbados Sunset, Christmas 1969
Watercolor 2022
Indisputably, there is nothing like a Caribbean sunset! Being so close to the equator, the sun sets in two to three minutes, and one must scurry to enjoy this daily array of colors.

Involving
self in life's
totality is
the aim.

Caribbean Seascape
Watercolor 2015
The Caribbean Sea is magical with its
crystal-clear blue abyss. Swimming in it makes
one feel completely at peace with the world.

Learning from the past aids us in accepting new experiences.

Llama in Machu Picchu, Peru
Watercolor 2023
A visit in 1968 to "The Lost City of the Incas" constructed in the 15th Century by the Incas, left an everlasting impression. No surprise it was named one of the New Seven Wonders of the World.

Experiencing
a simple day
with nature
is peaceful.

Mock Orange Blossoms
Watercolor 2015

The beautiful flowers on the Mock Orange bush are especially fragrant and leave a lifelong memory. The bush can be up to eight feet tall. The flowers are white, have a yellow center, and are about two inches across with four to five petals.

Creating
space for
others makes
a good
relationship.

Bromeliad in Cerro Altamira, Venezuela
Watercolor 2023
This radiant bromeliad was discovered
while hunting for orchids with a friend in Cerro
Altamira in 1967. What a spectacular surprise!

Empowering individuals to live and love liberates us.

Ruby-Throated Hummingbird, Female II
Watercolor 2022
These very small birds hover around flower blossoms gathering nectar. They spend winters in Mexico, Central America, and northern South America. They start migration in September and return north starting in February. Encountering one is magical!

Trusting
our Creator
in everyday
life gives us
confidence.

Zinnia and Monarch
Watercolor 2019

The Monarch is said to be the most recognizable of butterflies. It lives where there is milkweed. The female lays eggs on the milkweed leaf and the hatched caterpillars eat only milkweed for a few weeks. Then they each spin a chrysalis and in a few more weeks a magnificent Monarch butterfly emerges from each chrysalis. A miracle!

Acquiring
self-esteem
helps us feel
good about
ourselves.

Blue-Crowned Motmot
Watercolor 2023
It is hard to forget this impressive colorful
bird spied in Guatemala.

*Appreciating
many
environments
amplifies
our minds.*

Guanaco in Chilean Patagonia Mountains
Watercolor 2023

Located at the end of South America and shared between Chile and Argentina, Patagonia spans more than a million square kilometers with magnificent lakes, forests, and ice fields. Guanaco, fox, and puma relish protection in this area. It was a magical splendor in 1970. United Nations Educational, Scientific and Cultural Organization (UNESCO) has named the *Los Glaciares* National Park a World Heritage Site.

Accepting friendships is one of life's greatest gifts.

Three Red Poppies
Watercolor 2023
This Red Poppy grows wild, is small and fragile, but it is a very popular wildflower.

Taking
time to
make my
soul happy
is my desire.

Pico Bolívar, Venezuela
Watercolor 2015
Pico Bolívar in the Andes of southwestern
Venezuela has an altitude of over 16,000 feet, The
cable car views to Pico Espejo left magnificent
memories as well as a needed wool stocking cap
and mittens.

Shining your light may make a positive impact on the world.

Southern Lights in Cape Bruny, Tasmania, Australia
Watercolor 2023

The Southern Lights (*Aurora Australis*) emblazon the night sky with flashing shades of green, blue, purple, and red. The Southern Lights can be observed all year round, although most frequently during winter (May to August in Australia) and during the spring equinox in September. Bruny Island is about as far south as one can get to Antarctica to view this spectacular event.

Discovering "how to see" can be an awakening.

Long-Tailed Hummingbird
Watercolor 2015
The fascinating Long-Tailed Hummingbird (Sylph) is found in the eastern slopes of the Andes from Venezuela to Bolivia. They use their long tails for navigation.

Responding to love is the foundation of all creation.

Angel Falls - Canaima, Venezuela
Watercolor 2019
Angel Falls is the highest waterfall in the world plunging at almost 1000 meters. It was named for U.S. Pilot, Jimmie Angel who crash-landed his plane on a plateau nearby in 1937. Canaima National Park is a UNESCO World Heritage Site.

Comprehending
we are meant
for a life
of freedom
is a joy.

Tiger Swallowtail
Watercolor 2023
Tiger Swallowtails are stunning black and yellow butterflies with long tails. They are, reportedly, the second most recognized butterflies in the United States.

Caring for others is natural.

Mama and Kitty
Watercolor 2023
Mother cats and their kittens have a very close, intimate bond and the young are given great care for their first few months.

Knowing
that you are
unconditionally
loved makes
life easier.

Young Doe
Watercolor 2023
A daily faithful friend while living
in the Texas Hill Country.

Offering gratitude can be the greatest gift.

Poinsettia Salvaje
Watercolor 2020
Poinsettias grow wild in Central America and South America. Every one of its flowers is truly amazing.

Applauding the success of others is a pleasure.

Meadow Flowers
Watercolor 2023
As children, we delighted in picking field flowers for our mother.

Celebrating
the mystery
of life makes
me feel alive.

Fiji Sunrise
Watercolor 2023
Awakening to this site on January 2, 1987, made creation shine.

Observing
nature tells
us that life
is precious.

Yellow Rose II
Watercolor 2022

The yellow rose always makes one feel good: its yellow color evokes feelings of warmth, tenderness, and love. It is a precious gift, anytime.

Making time for yourself can be revitalizing.

Church in Heiligenblut, Austria
Watercolor 2022
Located in the eastern Alps, Heiligenblut is situated at the foot of the Grossglockner, the highest mountain in Austria: a breathtaking view! The church of St. Vincent is a favorite stop.

Believing
in someone
defines
his or her
worth.

Dusk at Salzburg Salt Mines
Watercolor 2016
This Alpine Village in the eastern Alps of Austria is Hallstatt, which means "Salt Settlement." These salt mines are the oldest in the world and have been in production since the second century. It has been selected as a World Heritage Site by UNESCO.

Helping
others reach
their full
potential is
my wish.

Mother Swan Carrying her Cygnets
Watercolor 2023
Mother swan keeps her little cygnets cozy and safe, teaches
them to find food and swim. She carries them on her back, so they
stay warm until their feathers grow.

Hoping
in the future
helps us live
creatively in
the present.

Sunrise in Tobago
Watercolor 2023
Another day brought in with glory!

Living
every
moment to
its fullest is
a delight.

Ripe Cherries
Watercolor 2023
What a pleasure to pick voluptuous cherries in Door County, Wisconsin and take them home for fresh fruit or pies.

Being
in the
present
moment
can make
life more
meaningful.

Hydrangeas in The Azores
Watercolor 2023
Gorgeous hydrangeas are everywhere on Portugal's Islands of The Azores. There are fences of hydrangeas as far as one can see. A sight to behold! June was an optimal month for viewing.

Enjoying
the magic of
springtime
is a
yearly joy.

Lupinus texensis
Texas Bluebonnet

Oenothera speciosa
Pink Evening Primrose

Coreopsis lanceolata

Castilleja
Indian Paintbrush

An exhibition of Texas wildflowers in watercolors from 2021.

Realizing
that nature
is a song
sung to us is
a treasure.

Spring Crocuses
Watercolor 2016
Crocuses peeking through some snow is a true sign of spring and a real challenge to the ending of winter. These flowers are always greeted with a big welcome and fascination!

Claiming
your worth
and value
does not
depend on
anyone else.

The Dolomites
Watercolor 2023

The Dolomites with their jagged pinnacles are in the Alps of northeastern Italy. They are a magical delight for hikers and skiers. The name is from the carbonate rock dolomite that make up the peaks. The rock was named for the 18th-century French geologist, Dolomieu. The Dolomite Mountains were declared a World Heritage Site by UNESCO.

Revealing nature's beauty in full color is profound.

Sugar Maple Leaf
Watercolor 2012

Maple Leaves II
Watercolor 2023

Mountain Ash Leaves
Watercolor 2023

Aspen Leaves
Watercolor 2023

Autumn's wonder in full display.

*Sharing
our
knowledge
is generous.*

Great Barrier Reef
Watercolor 2023

The Great Barrier Reef along the coast of Queensland, Australia is the world's largest coral reef system. A glass bottom boat facilitated the enjoyment of thousands of fascinating marine life. The Great Barrier Reef is a UNESCO World Heritage Site.

Being chosen indicates a special bond.

Fritz
Pastels 1974
Boxers are affectionate dogs and want to be social. The more positive attention given to them, the more they return. These are treasured memories of an excellent pet and a true friend.

Loving is our true treasure.

Christ the Redeemer, Rio de Janeiro
Watercolor 2023
This awesome statue viewed on Mount Corcovado in Rio de Janeiro, Brazil was completed in 1931 and is 98 feet tall with extended arms of 92 feet. It was named one of the New Seven Wonders of the World.

Bibliography

Begazo, Alfredo. 2020. "Hummingbird Identification: An Illustrated Guide to All 14 North American Species." Avian Report. August 23, 2020.

Centre, UNESCO World Heritage. n.d. "Hallstatt-Dachstein / Salzkammergut Cultural Landscape." UNESCO World Heritage Centre. https://whc.unesco.org/en/list/806.

———. n.d. "Los Glaciares National Park." UNESCO World Heritage Centre. https://whc.unesco.org/en/list/145/Los.

———. n.d. "The Dolomites." UNESCO World Heritage Centre. https://whc.unesco.org/en/list/1237.

———. n.d. "UNESCO World Heritage Centre - Document - CHRIST the REDEEMER from DONA MARTA BELVEDERE." UNESCO World Heritage Centre. https://whc.unesco.org/en/documents/117439.

"Species Profile: Blue-Crowned Motmot." n.d. Rainforest Alliance. https://www.rainforest-alliance.org/species/motmot.

The Editors of Encyclopedia Britannica. 2016. "Angel Falls | Waterfall, Venezuela." In *Encyclopædia Britannica*. https://www.britannica.com/place/Angel-Falls.

———. 2018. "Monarch Butterfly | Life Cycle, Caterpillar, Migration, & Facts." In *Encyclopædia Britannica*. https://www.britannica.com/animal/monarch-butterfly.

World, UNESCO. 2011. "Historic Sanctuary of Machu Picchu." Unesco.org. 2011. https://whc.unesco.org/en/list/274.

———. 2019. "Canaima National Park." Unesco.org. 2019. https://whc.unesco.org/en/list/701.

Printed in the United States
by Baker & Taylor Publisher Services